TO:

_____

FROM:

_____

DATE:

_____

JESUS
— IS FOR —
YOU
✝

STORIES OF GOD'S RELENTLESS LOVE

JUDAH SMITH

THOMAS NELSON
Since 1798

NASHVILLE · MEXICO CITY · RIO DE JANEIRO

Published in Nashville, Tennessee, by Thomas Nelson. Thomas Nelson is a registered trademark of HarperCollins Christian Publishing, Inc.

Interior Photography: © Shutterstock: pages i–vii,xiii–3,6–9,13–17,20–25,28–31,34–37, 40–45,48–51,54–59,64–67,69–73,76–79,82–87,90–93,98–103,106–113,116–121,124–127, 130–135,138–143,146–149,152–155,158–160

Published in association with the literary agency of Fedd & Company, Inc., P.O. Box 341973, Austin, TX 78734.

Thomas Nelson titles may be purchased in bulk for educational, business, fund-raising, or sales promotional use. For information, please e-mail SpecialMarkets@ThomasNelson.com.

ISBN-13: 978-0-7180-2310-2

Printed in China

5 16 17 18 19 DSC 6 5 4 3 2 1

In honor of my mom, Virginia Smith . . .
your strength inspires me daily.

Love has been perfected among us in this: that we may have boldness in the day of judgment; because as He is, so are we in this world.

When God
sees us,
He sees
Jesus.

CONTENTS

INTRODUCTION

My wife and I are the parents of three young children. We love them deeply, but we have discovered that they are the loudest children on the entire planet. I have no idea who they get that from.

As a father, one of my least favorite responsibilities is to be a referee. Not for sports—I'm fine with that. I'm talking about refereeing the controversies and contentions and conflicts that arise among these three very verbal offspring.

Things like who gets to eat the last piece of bacon.

Who gets to control the remote control.

Who gets to sit in the comfortable chair.

There's an easy answer to all of the above, of course: *Dad does*. That seems fair, right? Call it one of the perks of parenthood. It's a double benefit, because not only do I get that last strip of crispy fried calories; I also avoid the hours of evidence they are prepared to present and the inevitable cross-examining of the witnesses.

But deep inside, I know that parental selfishness won't work out well. I'm supposed to be an example of generosity. So instead, I find myself trying to be firm and loving and impartial and non-emotional and infinitely wise, which also doesn't work out that well because I am human and I will always give in to my daughter and her big blue eyes. Sorry, boys.

What my kids want to know in any argument is this: *Is Dad on my side? Is Dad for me . . . or against me?* They know that if Dad is on their side, the argument is over. Dad's approval means the debate is resolved and they have won.

As a pastor and speaker, I end up talking to a lot of people about spirituality. It's fascinating. Hearing their journeys and perspectives never gets old.

In these conversations, one thing I often hear is an underlying, almost subconscious assumption that God is *against* us. People don't usually say it that way, of course. But that's the attitude that comes across. *God is not on my side. God is not backing me up. God is not for me.*

I've been there myself more times than I can count. Maybe you have too. When we fail, when we stumble over the same temptations again and again, when we come face-to-face with our humanity, it's far too easy to think that God is as disappointed with us as we are with ourselves, to imagine God frustrated and frowning because our humanity is showing.

But that's not the God that Jesus reveals to us. Jesus came to earth and lived among us to demonstrate a God who cares. A God who loves us with such depth and devotion that He sent His own Son to save us. A God who knows exactly who we are and accepts us just the same. Jesus came to show us that God isn't against us—He is unconditionally and irrevocably *for* us.

This book is a collection of Bible verses, inspirational thoughts, and real-life stories all centered around the simple truth that Jesus is for you. I pray that as you peruse these pages, you will be reminded of His love, His acceptance, and His never-ending mercy and grace.

Jesus is for you. Can there be any greater source of strength and courage than that?

Judah Smith

The only thing that can fill the void is the scandalous, unconditional love of Jesus.

Restore to me the joy of your salvation.

—Psalm 51:12

It's not my salvation—
it's God's. I am not the
originator or the creator.
It's His work of grace.
It's His initiative.

Part 1

JESUS IS . . .

For by grace you have been saved through faith, and that not of yourselves; it is the gift of God, not of works, lest anyone should boast. For we are His workmanship, created in Christ Jesus for good works, which God prepared beforehand that we should walk in them.

—Ephesians 2:8–10 NKJV

Religion says: "Behave, believe, and then you will belong." The gospel says the opposite: "Belong, then believe, then behave." Another way of saying that is: "Amazing grace, great faith, and good works."

GRACE

My mother was saved back when she was a teenager, and she raised us in church. Going to church wasn't optional. We went! We went to church all day on Sunday—every Sunday. We went Friday nights, Wednesday nights . . . lots of nights. So I didn't really get a choice as a kid whether to serve Jesus. I was born into Jesus, you might say.

When I was young, I loved God and I loved the concept of church. I would play during the service until the preacher started; then I would tell my friends, "Quiet, I need to hear this." I'd tell the usher to get my friends in trouble if they weren't quiet.

But our church was full of rules, and you had to meet certain standards or requirements. It turns out that lots of those rules weren't in the Bible. They were just human ideas used to control people. Even at a young age, I could see that the rules were a lot of show. It was easy to look and act a certain way in front of people but be an entirely different person behind the scenes.

I used to view Jesus as a taskmaster. He was the mighty "I Am," whose goal was to control me. Fear kept me on the straight and narrow. If I messed up or didn't read the Bible enough one day, I felt damned to hell. I felt like Jesus was a dictator.

I accepted all of this as a kid, but at some point in life, God began tugging at me, helping me see that there is more to Him than I had been shown. I began to get to know God and Jesus for myself. I realized that God loves me regardless of my mistakes or whether I meet all the criteria or rules or standards people make up.

NOTHING I CAN DO OR SAY, OR BE OR NOT BE, WILL MAKE JESUS LOVE ME MORE OR LOVE ME LESS.

Now Jesus doesn't seem like a taskmaster to me—He is *my friend*. I like to call Him my homey. Before, there was this huge separation between us, like He was completely different from me and I was just supposed to be meek and lowly. But now I know that He loves me no matter what. Nothing I can do or say, or be or not be, will make Him love me more or love me less. He chases after me and pursues me. He's my friend and He has my back.

—Allen

For the grace of God has been revealed, bringing salvation to all people.

—Titus 2:11

Jesus embodied grace.
He oozed grace.
He *was* grace.

We have seen his glory, glory as of the only Son from the Father, full of grace and truth.

—John 1:14 ESV

Jesus was full of grace and truth. That means that grace and truth aren't enemies. They are on the same side. We don't need to balance grace with truth or truth with grace, because they are both personified in Jesus. If we just get more of Jesus, we will have both grace and truth.

THE TRUTH

I was raised in a Christian home, but I really didn't know Jesus personally. By the time I was thirteen or fourteen, I had begun looking for affirmation, identity, and self-worth in the wrong places. I began drinking and partying and got into some really bad relationships. When I was fourteen, I started dating a nineteen-year-old guy, and when I was eighteen, we moved in together.

In college, I met a Christian guy who introduced me to the gospel and Jesus. I was still living with my boyfriend and was dealing with a lot of brokenness. This Christian man amazed me because he respected and honored me. He introduced me to a new way of seeing myself by the way he treated me.

WHEN I MET JESUS, I FINALLY ENCOUNTERED A LOVE THAT DIDN'T ENSLAVE ME BUT INSTEAD SET ME FREE.

I realized that his actions were a result of his relationship with Jesus, and I began to study the Bible for myself. I finally discoverd that it wasn't about rules, regulations, or a religion to be followed. It was about a person: Jesus.

When I met Jesus, I finally encountered a love that didn't enslave me but instead set me free. I had never before understood the concept of love. I fell in love with Jesus as a response to His love for me.

My journey with Jesus began there, but I realized I couldn't do it alone—I needed community. I began attending a local church. I had been going for about two months when I met a woman who was one of the leaders of the church. She invited me to join the team of greeters who welcomed people as they arrived to church. With some trepidation, I agreed.

I loved it instantly.

I began to get more involved with other groups and activities in the church. And in all of this I discovered relationships—real, authentic relationships where I could be truly honest. I joined a small group and got to know some women in the church who became mentors to me. For the first time, I learned that honesty and accountability do not bring shame or guilt, but freedom and healing.

HONESTY AND ACCOUNTABILITY DO NOT BRING SHAME OR GUILT, BUT FREEDOM AND HEALING.

Because I was the one who had gotten my life into such a mess in the first place through my poor choices, I had believed that maybe Jesus didn't want to heal me. After all, my problems were my own fault. But He continued to show me that whether something bad happened to me or whether I made a bad decision myself, He wanted to heal me and set me free, and His grace was there for me time and time again.

Jesus is so faithful. And it's His work, not my own, that has led to my life being healed and whole.

I had known Jesus as my Savior for a long time . . . but now I know Him also as my healer.

—Diane

It's not about
how much
we love God.
It's about
how much
He loves us.

We love Him because He first loved us.

—1 John 4:19 NKJV

God's love is so extravagant and so inexplicable that He loved us before we were us. He loved us before we existed. He knew many of us would reject Him, hate Him, curse Him, rebel against Him. Yet He chose to love us. God loves us because He is love.

Though I walk through the valley of the shadow of death, I will fear no evil; for You are with me.

—Psalm 23:4 NKJV

Jesus is the resurrection and the life. Jesus is the victorious King of ages. Jesus rules and reigns, and He's sovereign, and He's big, and He's majestic, and He's strong, and He's able to help you with anything you are facing.

VICTORIOUS

Growing up, I never felt very gifted, at least not at anything tangible. That produced a lot of fear in my life. I didn't think God wanted to use me. I felt inadequate. These feelings escalated until my life became completely crippled by fear.

Despite these fears, I joined the intern program at my church. One night I heard a message about sin and the power of the cross. I remember thinking that it wasn't sin I needed to be saved from at that point. I needed to be saved from fear.

I ENCOUNTERED JESUS LIKE NEVER BEFORE. I REALIZED THE VAST GREATNESS OF THE CROSS AND WHAT JESUS HAD DONE FOR ME.

That night I encountered Jesus like never before. I realized the vast greatness of the cross and what Jesus had done for me. I finally saw that Jesus' death didn't conquer just the big sins. It also covered all the little things I struggled with, all my inadequacies and fears. I was set free that night.

Before that encounter, I often refused opportunities offered to me because I was too afraid to take them. I said no to everything. Now I am able to confidently say yes to the opportunities God gives me and to know that He will make me capable and give me everything I need.

God conquered everything for me. He loves me from the inside out. He chose me and He wants to use me for His kingdom.

GOD CONQUERED EVERYTHING FOR ME.

My focus used to be only on my own fear, but now I'm able to love Jesus, to focus on Him, and to love other people who are still trapped in fear themselves. I am free!

—Katie

Jesus didn't come to condemn the world; He came to save the world. If He thinks there is hope, if He believes in humanity, we should too.

"I want you to show mercy,
not offer sacrifices."

—Matthew 9:13

Jesus came to
reveal a God
who defines us
not by our actions
but by His love.

When we focus on His goodness, His power, and His grace, we are hardly even aware of what is happening, but we begin to change. We begin to be more like Jesus.

THE LIFE GIVER

Ten years ago, I was involved in some very dark relationships. It was a pattern in my life. I kept telling myself I would change, but the only changes I ever made were superficial. Nothing changed deep inside me.

I eventually found myself contemplating suicide. I realized I either had to change or I would die.

I ended up at church. The moment I stepped in, I felt something awesome in the atmosphere. You could breathe it and feel it.

The pastor was preaching about holiness. The darkness I had been living in was eating me up, and his message hit home. God is holy—I need to be holy. God touched my heart, and I wanted to change. I knew with certainty that the answer was to change, not to kill myself.

GOD TOUCHED MY HEART, AND I WANTED TO CHANGE.

When I decided to change, I turned 180 degrees: I left my old friends and those dark relationships. That was painful. I felt like it was just Jesus and me at that point. But it paid off.

The community at church accepted me and

supported me. Even though they knew the wrong things in my life, they still accepted me. God put people around me, and I am no longer alone. He planted me in a church where I am a member of a family. I couldn't ask for more.

Before Jesus got hold of my life, I refused to be involved with anything. I wanted to hide. But now He has given me so much that I *have* to give something. I can't keep it to myself! I volunteer every Sunday as a greeter at my church. I also do volunteer work with the elderly. If they are in pain and I cannot help them, I pray for them. Many have wanted to accept Jesus, and walking them through that at the end of their lives is really so amazing. I was not this person in the past, but *everything changed because of Jesus*.

—Marlette

EVERYTHING CHANGED BECAUSE OF JESUS.

Put on your new nature, and be renewed as you learn to know your Creator and become like him.

—Colossians 3:10

Jesus gave me a new way to be human. At the core of my being, I am holy, righteous, godly, compassionate, generous, loving, and sensitive. I have a new nature, and it mirrors the God who created me.

God is with us *because God is for us.* He's here to make sure we're taken care of. He's here to hook us up and back us up. He's here to provide, protect, and empower.

A GREAT HEALER

We have three boys. Liam is our youngest. While he was in the womb, there were no complications—both mother and baby were healthy. We anticipated soon holding him in our arms. But to everyone's shock, when Liam was born, he wasn't breathing.

One nurse kept saying, "It's gonna be okay," as the medical team performed CPR on Liam, but she looked very scared. We trusted that Jesus is our healer and knew that the only thing we could do was turn to God for help.

WE TRUSTED THAT JESUS IS OUR HEALER AND KNEW THAT THE ONLY THING WE COULD DO WAS TURN TO GOD FOR HELP.

The medical team was able to revive Liam, but the doctor told us he would probably have to remain in the hospital for several months. But every step of the way—in fact, almost every single day—Liam made astounding progress. One month after he was born, we took him home. It was an emotional day for us with plenty of excitement and happy tears. It was truly a day we were thankful for.

The whole ordeal made us realize how important our church is to us. We were so blessed by the way everybody came together and supported us during that time. They truly have been like a second family for us.

—Cory & Melissa

THE WHOLE ORDEAL MADE US REALIZE HOW IMPORTANT OUR CHURCH IS TO US.

God is not in a hurry to fix us. Our behavior is not His first priority. We are His first priority. Loving us is His main concern.

Therefore, since we have been made right in God's sight by faith, we have peace with God because of what Jesus Christ our Lord has done for us. Because of our faith, Christ has brought us into this place of undeserved privilege where we now stand, and we confidently and joyfully look forward to sharing God's glory.

—Romans 5:1–2

Grace is Jesus,
and Jesus
is enough.

OUR GREAT COMFORTER

Several years ago, we received the middle-of-the-night phone call every parent dreads: our daughter Stephanie had been in a car accident. Police officers came to our door, and an officer drove me to the hospital while my husband, Don, woke up our three other children and prepared to follow in our car.

I was praying on the way to the hospital, and when the police officer driving me noticed, she offered to pray with me. So we prayed together.

When we reached the hospital, Stephanie was already in the operating room. Soon Don arrived with the kids. They had passed right by the scene of the accident and had seen the mangled wreckage and the flashing lights of emergency vehicles. They knew the accident was bad.

We waited while the doctors tried to save Stephanie. They had revived her several times on the way to the hospital, but they couldn't stabilize her. Eventually we were given the news that she had passed. That was so hard.

By then our pastor and his wife had arrived to be with us. I couldn't handle the thought of going in and officially identifying my daughter's body, so Don and our pastor did it.

We went home and began to experience the whole gamut of emotions and grief. Our church community was really supportive. They brought us meals for several days, until after the memorial service.

We continued going to church and letting God heal us. Everyone grieves differently, and we can't get inside each other's skin. But Jesus can. He was able to help Don where he was and meet me where I was as a mom. We tried to rest, even as we walked through the process—and it was a process.

I MADE THE CHOICE TO TRUST GOD. AND HE HELPED US.

During that time, we learned how truly important community is. We can't shut people out. We need to be open and allow them to grieve with us.

As God came alongside, He began to heal us very gently, with time and with people around us. At first I remember thinking, *I don't think I can go on. This is so hard.* But I made the choice to trust God, even though my emotions were all over the place. And He helped us.

There are times, even now, when the wound comes back, and I can touch it again. But Jesus has been so faithful. I'm ever so thankful for that.

—Pat & Don

The Bible calls death the final enemy. It's a bigger enemy than sickness, doubt, fear, sin, poverty, or pain. Jesus conquered this final enemy in the resurrection. That means we don't have to fear anything—even death.

"How often I have wanted to gather your children together as a hen protects her chicks beneath her wings, but you wouldn't let me."

—Matthew 23:37

Jesus isn't standing aloof, yelling at us to climb out of our pits and clean ourselves up so we can be worthy of Him. He is wading waist-deep into the muck of life, weeping with the broken, rescuing the lost, and healing the sick.

That is the gospel:
God is with us.
Jesus is God in the
flesh, here on earth,
hanging out with
sinful people.

A VERY PRESENT HELP

When I was nine, my mother died and my father had a stroke. It was very rough—even more so because it was so unexpected and happened all at once. When I was growing up, we were so poor that I often ate only when I had school meals or when I could get myself invited to a friend's house for a meal. Then I would eat everything I could.

My mother was half-Thai, but she only spoke to us in English. My dad was full Thai, but he didn't speak English. Since I never learned Thai, I grew up unable to communicate with my dad. I was never able to get advice from him or learn from him how to deal with issues as a child and a teenager. That was a tough spot for a young man to be in. I felt so alone.

When I got older, I joined the army. I was in the service for about five years, including a tour in Iraq. The military is a challenging environment. God isn't really talked about; you do things on your own. I had gone to church with my mom as a child. During my time in the military, I lost touch with those Christian roots.

JESUS SHOWED ME I DON'T HAVE TO DO IT ALONE.

But seeds had been sown during those childhood years in church, even if I didn't know it, and they eventually bore fruit. God led me out of the military. It was like He said to me, "You followed the call of the nation, but I have something bigger for you—the call of God."

I began to go back to church, and I realized that Jesus had been with me the whole time. He had been caring for me and loving me even though I hadn't seen it.

That's why it really hits my heart when I see people trying to do it alone, to get through life alone. God doesn't want you to do it alone!

As my faith grew, I became really passionate about God. I wanted to get involved helping others, so I started cooking for the volunteers at church, especially the media team. On Sundays, I get up at 7:00 a.m. and bake. Then I put food in the slow cooker. I spend about three hours cooking and then take the food to the church. The smell attracts people, and they come from the cameras and the studio rooms at random times to gather around and eat. I love that I can help foster this sense of community and remind people that they are loved and appreciated and are not forgotten.

I grew up feeling alone and without someone to turn to, but now I'm part of a wonderful church family. Jesus showed me I don't have to do it alone. I'm loved and cared for. The Lord is my strength and my rock. He never left me. He has always been there and always will be.

—Billy

What is your life? It is even a vapor that appears for a little time and then vanishes away.

—James 4:14 NKJV

The meaning of life
is not found in this life.
Life is not about being
happy. It's about God.
Focusing on God brings
meaning to our lives.

"For God so loved the world that He gave His only begotten Son, that whoever believes in Him should not perish but have everlasting life."

—John 3:16 NKJV

Jesus spent His time with the needy, the helpless, and the depraved. He came down to their level because they could never rise to His. He wasn't out to prove how good He was or how bad they were. He just wanted to offer them hope.

THE KEEPER OF THE SPARROWS

Growing up, I suffered through a number of traumatizing experiences and really difficult times. My parents had a lot of marital issues, so I grew up hearing them fighting constantly and knowing that they didn't trust each other.

I didn't have any control over most of these circumstances. I tried escaping through partying and drinking, but it didn't help. I was confused and very depressed.

It wasn't until I found myself at my lowest low that I called out to Jesus. I remember being on the floor in my room saying, "Whatever it is that You have, I want to receive it." I didn't know if God would even answer, but I knew I needed Him.

Something changed in me that day. For the first time, I felt hope. With the help of friends and my church, I started my journey with Jesus. I began praying and believing that Jesus is my joy, my refuge, my restorer, and my healer.

GOD IS BIGGER THAN MY CIRCUMSTANCES.

And everything started to change.

I was able not only to deal with the circumstances in my life but also to move past them and actually grow from them. I realized that God is bigger than my circumstances and that, even though I can't control certain things around me, I can trust in the One who can. It gave me hope and faith.

Others noticed the changes in my life. My vocabulary was less negative. I felt stronger and more confident. I was more secure in who I am because of Jesus, who lives in me. My relationship with my parents improved.

Now my passion is to help other people who are going through similar situations. I don't want to just give them a how-to of what you need to do to be happy but to help them see who Jesus really is and how He can transform their lives. Jesus is truly my joy and fulfillment.

—Natalie

MY PASSION IS TO HELP OTHER PEOPLE SEE WHO JESUS REALLY IS AND HOW HE CAN TRANSFORM THEIR LIVES.

Endless crowds stand around [the king],
but then another generation grows
up and rejects him, too. So it is all
meaningless—like chasing the wind.

—Ecclesiastes 4:16

God is not ambiguous. He is not ethereal or undefined. God reveals Himself in Jesus. Jesus is the awesomeness of God, the glory of God, and the ultimate manifestation of God. He is God with skin on.

Part 2

JESUS GIVES . . .

Then Jesus said, "Come to me, all of you who are weary and carry heavy burdens, and I will give you rest. Take my yoke upon you. Let me teach you, because I am humble and gentle at heart, and you will find rest for your souls. For my yoke is easy to bear, and the burden I give you is light."

—Matthew 11:28–30

Jesus wants us to come to the end of ourselves so we can discover the grace God freely offers through Jesus.

A TRUE HOME

I was born and raised in a religion other than Christianity. On the positive side, I was brought up with morals, guidance, community, and a vast amount of Bible knowledge. But I was also instilled with rules, boundaries, punishment, guilt, shame, and isolation. I lived in fear of doing wrong and embarrassing my family. I was taught the Scriptures in negative ways, and I was made to feel like no matter what I did, it was never good enough for God.

My mom had medical problems most of my life. Then, when I was sixteen, my dad was diagnosed with terminal cancer. Overwhelmed by this new diagnosis and an already sick mother, I tried to turn to God. But despite all my efforts, I never felt that Jesus was my friend. I never experienced that kind of relationship where I could talk to Him about my issues.

One week after my eighteenth birthday, my mom died unexpectedly. I felt so alone. She was the glue of our family. She was my best friend, and I miss her every day.

She and I had been the strong ones in our religion, but now God was the last person I wanted to cry to. I started to feel like He was a mean, cruel God. I resented Him . . . then I hated Him . . . and eventually I quit believing in Him completely. I left religion, I left God, and I didn't look back.

Eight months after my mom died, I met the man who is now my husband, Justin. He believed in God and had been to church at one point, but he wasn't religious, which worked out well for me.

Just shy of our wedding, when I was twenty, my dad passed away from cancer. The church my family had been part of had already decided that we were sinners, that we were people who didn't walk in the ways of God. They forbid us to talk to any of our family or friends. So when I needed help the most, I felt like neither God nor the church was there for me.

Fast-forward to the present. I am twenty-three now. A little over a month ago, my husband's family invited us to their church. We made a deal. We would attend once and keep an open mind. But if we didn't like it, they would leave us alone.

At first I was terribly uncomfortable. *Wait a minute. They serve coffee? Is that woman wearing jeans? Why is there a stage full of instruments?* Then a man in camo skinny jeans, boots, a white shirt buttoned to the top, and thick black-rimmed glasses stepped up to the microphone and began to talk about God, Jesus, and love.

THAT MORNING, I FOUND OUT WHO GOD REALLY IS.

GOD LOVED ME EVEN WHEN I DIDN'T LOVE HIM, EVEN WHEN I TURNED FROM HIM AND HATED HIM. HE HAD NEVER LEFT MY SIDE.

That morning, I found out who God really is. I was moved to tears. The message was about God's love—not just for anyone, but for me specifically. I was leaning forward, hanging on every word, convinced that this was for me.

I realized that the entire time I had been angry with God, He had been there for me. He loved me even when I didn't love Him, even when I turned from Him and hated Him. He had never left my side.

I had read the Bible before, but it was like I was hearing God's Word for the first time. It's not about rules and discipline and hate. It's about love, forgiveness, and sacrifice. God gave up His only Son, Jesus, knowing full well what was in store for Him, and He did it out of love for me and you. Wow.

Since that first Sunday, my husband and I have both been hooked. *Obsessed* may be a more appropriate word. For the first time in twenty-three years, I actually feel a bond with God. Our lives have changed so much. My personal relationship with God is incredible. I continue to learn new things every day. Jesus is with me, holding my hand when I need Him and letting me cry on His shoulder. He never judges; He simply shows love and patience.

I am happy to spend the rest of my days knowing that Jesus is with me: loving me, forgiving me, encouraging me. He is the best friend I'll ever have.

—Alicia

JESUS IS WITH ME, HOLDING MY HAND WHEN I NEED HIM AND LETTING ME CRY ON HIS SHOULDER. HE NEVER JUDGES; HE SIMPLY SHOWS LOVE AND PATIENCE.

And the Lord—who is the Spirit—makes us more and more like him as we are changed into his glorious image.
—2 Corinthians 3:18

Once Jesus is the focal point—once He is the culmination of life and the pinnacle of our existence—everything else makes sense. Life becomes simple again. Priorities fall into place, and peace, joy, and rest return.

How beautiful on the mountains are the feet of the messenger who brings good news, the good news of peace and salvation, the news that the God of Israel reigns!

—Isaiah 52:7

When we grasp the goodness of God, when we are full of the joy of His salvation, we won't be able to keep our mouths shut. We will tell others about Jesus because He has changed our lives.

GOOD NEWS IN DARK PLACES

I am a minister in a church outside Joplin, Missouri. A man who had attended our church a few times was sent to prison, and I visited him there several times. On one of those visits I gave him a book called *Jesus Is _____* to read.

He was recently released from prison and came to our church. I asked him if he liked the book. His response was amazing.

He told me he read the whole book in two days. Then he began telling some of the other inmates about it. Many of them wanted to read it too. Soon, so many people were trying to get their hands on it that he ended up writing down all their names and checking the book out to people as if it were a library book.

He said the environment in the prison began to change. Inmates started coming up to him talking about Jesus and how excited they were about the grace He offers.

When he was released from prison, he left the book there, still in circulation. He said he has no doubt that lives in that prison are still being changed.

—Johnny

Jesus is
the point
of life.

"I bring you good news that will bring great joy to all people."

—Luke 2:10

Jesus and joy
are always a
package deal.
And it's not just
your average joy—
it's great joy.

"I am the good shepherd; I know my own sheep, and they know me, just as my Father knows me and I know the Father. So I sacrifice my life for the sheep."

—John 10:14–15

Jesus' passion
was looking for lost,
lonely souls and
bringing them
home to God.

RELIEF FROM WORRY

My dad left my mom and me when I was four years old, and I've led a troubled life ever since. The people who know me probably wouldn't consider me troubled. To them I'm the cheerful girl who is always loud and happy and active in church.

But I went through a lot of negative things with family, friends, and relationships. I've struggled with my share of vices as well. Deep inside I have always longed for relief and always felt like something was missing

Life has been especially hard this year. I got laid off from work, experienced a family tragedy, had my heart broken, was betrayed by a friend, and got into a car accident. I've felt so far from the Lord. I got mad at Him actually. I questioned why He gave me this kind of life—and why I keep failing even when trying my hardest to succeed.

But my whole perspective on life has changed. I used to think the Lord wanted me to be the best person, the best daughter, and the best Christian possible. I tried so hard to be the best at

I DON'T HAVE TO BE THE BEST. I CAN JUST BE *ME*. THE WAY GOD MADE ME.

everything. I thought that God was giving me a chance to turn my life around.

And He was—but I was doing it wrong.

I realized that I don't have to be the best. I can just be *me*. The way God made me.

I began to understand that Jesus wants to experience everything with me. He wants to share every single moment of happiness and sadness. He wants me to take a step back, to stay by His side, and to allow Him to show me how awesome life with Him is.

All that time I was searching for happiness, love, and care? I was looking in the wrong place. All I needed to do was look to Jesus. He is my happiness, and He is my love.

I'm sure I'll still be the emotional person I am. I'll still have difficult and stressful days. But instead of looking to the world for relief, I now know that I need only look to Jesus. He is grace and He is relief. I know that when I do that, everything else will follow.

JESUS IS GRACE AND HE IS RELIEF.

My circumstances haven't changed, yet I have never been happier and more at peace. Now I know where to turn and whom to hold on to.

Now I know who Jesus is in my life: *Jesus is my everything.*

—Dani

For you died to this life, and your real life is hidden with Christ in God. And when Christ, who is your life, is revealed to the whole world, you will share in all his glory.

—Colossians 3:3–4

There is only one person God is impressed with, and that is Jesus. If you want to impress God, trust in Jesus. When you trust in Jesus, your life is hidden in Christ. It's wrapped up in Jesus. When God looks at you, He sees His Son. That's when He says, "Wow!"

"There is more joy in heaven over one lost sinner who repents and returns to God than over ninety-nine others who are righteous and haven't strayed away!"

—Luke 15:7

Even in our darkest moments of sin and self-centeredness, God still loves us. No matter what. And the moment He sees an inkling of repentance, He goes crazy.

NEW LIFE

Growing up, I never really had a personal relationship with Jesus. When I moved away to college, I started drinking and doing drugs. It eventually turned into something I couldn't control.

I began to steal to support my habit. I didn't want to, but in that state of mind, I believed it was necessary. My addiction controlled everything I did.

The first time I did methamphetamine, I went out of my mind. Totally psychotic. I ended up robbing a bank. At the time, robbing the bank seemed like a completely moral choice because I needed and wanted something.

MY ADDICTION CONTROLLED EVERYTHING I DID.

That act changed the course of my life. I went to jail, which led to a cycle of spending time in institutions and then ending up back on the street and then back in jail. But nothing changed in my heart.

One day, out of the blue, the thought hit me that I should go to Seattle, Washington. I packed my bags and hopped on a Greyhound bus. When I arrived, I walked to the library and started looking up homeless shelters on the Internet.

I realized that a woman sitting across from me at another computer was staring at me intently. When I made eye contact, she said, "Do you know that Jesus loves you?"

She ended up taking me off to the side, where she prayed with me for a long time. She gave me a card with information about her church.

JESUS CHRIST GAVE ME THE LOVE AND THE HOPE THAT THE WORLD COULDN'T OFFER ME.

I went to the church the next day, and I immediately felt at home. I submitted my life to Christ, and I finally received the healing I'd found nowhere else. Jesus Christ gave me the love and the hope that the world couldn't offer me. All I can say is: Jesus is my Redeemer.

—Brad

Loving God means keeping his commandments,
and his commandments are not burdensome.
For every child of God defeats this evil world,
and we achieve this victory through our faith.

—1 John 5:3–4

When we let
Jesus love us
and learn to
love Him in
return, holiness
happens.

Dear friends, we are already God's children, but he has not yet shown us what we will be like when Christ appears. But we do know that we will be like him, for we will see him as he really is.

—1 John 3:2

So let us come boldly to the throne of our gracious God. There we will receive his mercy, and we will find grace to help us when we need it most.

—Hebrews 4:16

If we have faith in Jesus and His work on the cross, then we are as righteous right now as we ever need to be. We can't add to it, and we can't take away from it. We are righteous enough to walk into heaven, right up to God's throne, and ask Him for whatever we need.

A NEW BEGINNING

I'm twenty-two years old. Three years ago, my life was going well. I was a Bible school graduate, I had a job, and I was a worship leader at my church. I felt like everything was falling into place at the right time.

Then I was raped.

It was shattering. I had committed myself to God. I had been faithful. Now what I had saved for so long had been stolen from me. The realization that what I had lost could not be regained hit me like a ton of bricks.

I told a couple in my church what had happened, but I didn't go to the police or tell my parents. I just wanted to forget about it forever.

Then my parents found an emergency contraception package in my purse. I told them what had happened to me. My mom supported me, but my dad looked me in the eye and said, "I don't believe you." That messed me up.

THE REALIZATION THAT WHAT I HAD LOST COULD NOT BE REGAINED HIT ME LIKE A TON OF BRICKS.

Life got even worse. The next week I lost my job. I was at rock bottom.

I left church and isolated myself for six months. I felt like God had left me, although in hindsight I can see now that He held me through every moment. Eventually, I recommitted my life to God and started going back to church.

But I wasn't healed. Some days were okay, but others were like a "throwback Thursday" picture, with me stuck on the same picture of my past.

Then I got Judah Smith's book *Jesus Is* _____. I couldn't put it down. Every page began tying up loose ends in my unraveled life.

JESUS IS EVERYTHING I WAS LOOKING FOR.

Now I'm standing here, staring right into the eyes of my Jesus. He is everything I was looking for.

I realize now that I was trying to earn, to deserve, and to be good enough to finally feel "worthy" and regain a normal life. This book was what I needed. It reintroduced me to Jesus and showed me that it was okay to bring down all the walls. I was able to let myself fall absolutely in love with Him.

I'm leading worship again, but from a different heart. Praise and worship are so powerful when you are in love with Jesus! I'm excited to keep living a life that points people to Him and encouraging them to know Him better.

JESUS IS A NEW BEGINNING.

It's so simple. And it just keeps getting better.

Jesus is a new beginning.

—Michelle

People who simply follow a list of laws are not in awe of God. They are bound by rules and regulations and duty. But when they fall in love with the awesomeness of God, and when they see His glory and His goodness, rules become secondary.

"Anyone who has seen me
has seen the Father!"

—John 14:9

If you want to know what God thinks of you, or what God would say about your sin, or how God would respond if He were face-to-face with you, just look at Jesus, and you'll know.

A WAY OUT

My family went to church as I was growing up, but to me church was just boring. I was usually the kid throwing spit wads at people from the back row. I wanted to hang out with the kids who liked to party. I rebelled at home and ran away a lot. When I say *a lot*, I'm talking about twenty to thirty times—and not just for a couple hours either. I'd disappear for days.

In sixth grade I started smoking cigarettes. It made me look like a tough guy, and I liked that admiration from my peers. I smoked weed for the first time just after finishing sixth grade. It became a daily habit for me that summer and on into middle school. In high school I just got worse—drinking, skipping classes, even showing up to class reeking of marijuana. That was me, Zach the stoner.

IT WAS LIKE THERE WAS SOMETHING IN ME THAT COULD BE FILLED ONLY BY SOMETHING OTHER THAN THE DRUGS AND ALCOHOL AND COUNTERFEIT LOVE THAT DEFINED MY LIFE.

In my senior year I tried cocaine, and after I graduated it became a habit. My buddies and I would spend hundreds of dollars a weekend doing coke, going to strip clubs, and drinking.

I hung out with tough guys that nobody wanted to mess with, and we used to get into fights with people at bars and beat them up. I enjoyed it. But at the same time, I felt empty. It was like there was something in me that could be filled only by something other than the drugs and alcohol and counterfeit love that defined my life.

I remained heavily into cocaine. I spent time in treatment centers and in jail. Then one night I tried crystal meth. I fell in love with it. It soon controlled me. I sold crack and was a security guard for escorts to support my meth habit. I broke into homes and cars, and I eventually started stealing credit card numbers by breaking into mailboxes.

One day I passed out in the car in my parents' driveway with a bag full of stolen mail. My parents had had enough and decided to call the cops. About six hours before all of this happened, I had been sitting in the house feeling completely lost. I had cried out to God, *If You're real, save me. I need Your help.*

I HAD CRIED OUT TO GOD, *IF YOU'RE REAL, SAVE ME. I NEED YOUR HELP.*

Well, His idea of saving me was my parents

calling the cops. So I ran down the street to the church I grew up in to hide from the police. While they were looking for me, sirens blaring, I heard a quiet voice saying to me, "This is the answer to your prayers. This is Me. Turn yourself in."

THE THING ABOUT JESUS IS THAT HE DIDN'T WAIT FOR ME TO GET MY LIFE IN ORDER. HE MET ME IN MY MESS.

So I did. The sheriff arrested me and put me in the police cruiser. But rather than take me to jail, he took me to my parents. And he arranged for me to enter a faith-based treatment center. I met Jesus there.

The thing about Jesus is that He didn't wait for me to get my life in order. He met me in my mess. He made me clean by taking my filthiness and wickedness and giving me His righteousness. He gave me joy and peace.

I still have issues, but God doesn't see my issues. When He looks at me, He sees Jesus. And when He sees Jesus, He sees perfect righteousness and holiness.

My past was full of hurt and shame. I tried to find healing with drugs and alcohol and sex. But the only thing that can fill that void is the unconditional, scandalous love of Jesus. He has given me peace and joy and has released me from shame.

I'm so thankful for my parents. They prayed for me for years. They lost sleep and gave up meals to pray for me. We serve a God whose arm is never short. When the time was right, I cried out to Him and He set me free from my sin. That's how He works.

—Zach

GOD DOESN'T SEE MY ISSUES. WHEN GOD LOOKS AT ME, HE SEES JESUS.

"I have come to call not those who think they are righteous, but those who know they are sinners."

—Matthew 9:13

Jesus made
a point of
seeking out
sinners and
befriending
them.

Who is this God with such layers of mercy and such amazing, great love? Who is this God who seeks out people who are dead and brings them to life, not because of their merit or their potential but because He is full of mercy and love?

"And be sure of this: I am with you always, even to the end of the age."

—Matthew 28:20

Jesus will never leave us. He will never abandon us. He will never give up on us. Jesus is always here.

THE STRENGTH TO GO ON

Seven years ago, my husband, Jonathan, had a massive stroke. We took him to the hospital immediately, but three days later he passed away.

We have two young children, and the children and I went through a time of great darkness at that point. It had all happened so suddenly. There was no preparation, and we didn't even get to say good-bye.

I BEGAN TO SEE THAT GOD WOULD SHOW US HOW TO GO ON. EVEN IN THE MIDST OF ALL THAT CHAOS, GOD WAS STILL IN CONTROL.

It was so difficult for us to understand why this had happened. I read the Bible and I read other books, looking for answers. Slowly I began to see that God would show us how to go on. Even in the midst of all that chaos, God was still in control.

Even now, it's painful when I see intact families. I see dads picking up their children and frolicking around. My kids aren't able to have those types of experiences that are so normal for other families, which has been challenging.

But time after time, God comforts me with

reminders that it's okay. I can't do all the things for my kids that Jonathan would have done, but God has them in His hands.

God is good. It took me a while to figure out how to say that again. But God is good, and He is so faithful.

—Kelly

Then Jesus wept.

—John 11:35

Jesus doesn't scorn our grief. He weeps with us. Our sorrow arouses His compassion.

"I am the resurrection and the life. Anyone who believes in me will live, even after dying. Everyone who lives in me and believes in me will never ever die."

—John 11:25–26

Jesus brings life out of death. He brings hope out of sorrow. He turns our mourning into joy. Jesus is there for us when we need Him most—whether we know it or not and whether we appreciate it or not.

Part 3

JESUS IS THERE WHEN . . .

"'We must celebrate with a feast, for this son of mine was dead and has now returned to life. He was lost, but now he is found.' So the party began."

—Luke 15:23–24

Being a son or daughter has nothing to do with being worthy. We are sons and daughters of God by birth, not by worth. That's why Jesus says we must be born again. We must be birthed.

WE'VE MESSED UP—BIG

I knew about God when I was growing up, but I didn't know Him personally. Jesus was just somebody from the past, somebody my parents believed in. Even if God was real, I was sure I didn't need Him. I knew a lot of successful people who weren't Christians, and I was confident I could handle life on my own. I could be successful, moral, and happy without following restrictive rules I didn't believe in anyway.

Then, in a moment, my life turned upside down. I had spent the weekend partying and drinking, and I was heading home. I pulled out onto the freeway and accelerated to fifty-five miles per hour—and suddenly I lost consciousness.

AT THAT MOMENT, I NEEDED GOD.

I woke up in a ditch. I was facing the wrong way. Then I saw people gathered around someone lying on the grass with a helmet on.

I had hit a motorcyclist. I watched in shock as someone tried unsuccessfully to find a pulse.

All my ideology about life being better without God had been a dead end—a lie. At that moment, I needed Him. In that moment of tragedy, my stubbornness was kicked out of me, and I no longer wanted to do life without Him.

I failed the Breathalyzer. I was facing a trial and maybe jail time.

I began meeting with a pastor that week. He just loved on me like a brother. When he asked if I wanted to ask Jesus into my heart, I said yes—and suddenly it all came out, everything that had been bottled up inside me. I started bawling my eyes out. The experience was more intense than any drug I'd ever taken, but in a good way.

I was still scared, but I now knew that I had a friend—Jesus. And this friend wouldn't just write letters to me in prison—He would be right there with me.

I did end up going to prison. While there, I finally reconnected with my family. I had spent years thinking I hated them, but I was amazed by their support, first during my sentencing and later while I was in prison. They visited, and we would have long conversations about their lives. It was awesome.

JESUS HAD ALWAYS BEEN THERE, WAITING FOR ME TO COME BACK.

I was able to go to college while in prison. I learned the Web development skills that got me the job I have today. I joined a church, and despite my fears that I'd be seen as a monster, I was accepted into that community. I even met my wife there.

Jesus to me is like the father to his prodigal son—and I am that son. Jesus had always been there, waiting for me to come back, and He will always be there. Jesus is a second chance.

—Kyle

God is
a God
of second
chances.

Have mercy on me, O God, because of your unfailing love. Because of your great compassion, blot out the stain of my sins. . . . For I recognize my rebellion; it haunts me day and night.

—Psalm 51:1, 3

Jesus befriends
the worst
of sinners,
so Jesus
befriends me.

"For I know the plans I have for you," says the LORD. "They are plans for good and not for disaster, to give you a future and a hope."

God is with us, and He is for us. This is the gospel. So no matter what I go through, He is with me and He is for me. He is on my side.

AN IDEA SEEMS CRAZY

Several years ago, I attended a business conference at our church called the School of Generosity. While I was there, I felt the Holy Spirit telling me to start a business selling my mom's English toffee.

I rejected the idea immediately. For one thing, neither my wife nor I has a business background. My education was in criminal justice, and my wife is a nurse. For another, I was battling cancer at the time and was in the middle of yearlong intensive chemotherapy treatment.

But the nudging from the Holy Spirit didn't go away. My wife, Kendra, and I sat down together and prayed about it. We listed all the reasons not to start a business. There were quite a few. But the one statement that countered all those reasons was simple: If God is for us, who can be against us? If God had really called us to start this business, He would make it successful.

IF GOD IS FOR US, WHO CAN BE AGAINST US?

We really didn't know what we were doing. We still don't! We're basically toffee fools. But we're continually amazed by how God gives us the wisdom, the tools, and the people we need to help us.

From the beginning, our goal has been to bless

others through our business. The business exists to make money for eternal significance. Of course, we need to earn enough money for our family, but that's not the primary reason for the business. Helping people is.

GOD GIVES US THE WISDOM, THE TOOLS, AND THE PEOPLE WE NEED TO HELP US.

Generosity isn't just about money. It's giving of yourself to others, whether it's your finances or emotional support or advice or encouragement.

The desire to give is what motivates us. Every time we face challenges with the business, we remember that our reason for existence is to bless others. That gives our work a greater significance and motivates us to keep going forward and continue expanding.

Jesus is generosity. God so loved the world that He *gave*. There is no way we could possibly outgive Him. He has healed my body, and He provides for our needs. As we walk through the many unknowns, Jesus is our Prince of Peace.

JESUS IS GENEROSITY.

—Trevor

"Don't be dejected and sad, for the joy of the LORD is your strength!"

—Nehemiah 8:10

God wants you to be happy, but joy has to be first found in God. Joy has to be first found in the good news of Jesus Christ. And when joy is found there, you'll find joy in everything else.

The law was given through Moses; grace and truth came through Jesus Christ.

—John 1:17 ESV

Grace is more than a principle, more than an idea, more than a doctrine or dogma, more than a cover-up for sin. Grace is a person. And His name is Jesus.

WE FOLLOW HIS WILL

We own a tax advisory company and a wealth advisory company. One day we found out that our church was going to run a fourteen-week program for business leaders. After some hesitation (it was the busiest time of year for one of our businesses), we decided to attend.

One of the most important things we learned was to carve out some time with God each morning. We learned to just be still and quiet instead of thinking about our e-mails or the next tasks we needed to accomplish. Those early morning times with God became precious to us.

GOD WAS DOING SOMETHING IN US PERSONALLY. HE WAS CHANGING OUR PERSPECTIVE.

We didn't see a lot of financial blessing or prosperity during that time. In fact, the six months surrounding the course were the worst months our business had experienced in twelve years of operation.

But God was doing something in us personally. He was changing our perspective.

During our morning prayer times, we began to

get past the idea of praying just to get something from God, and instead we found ourselves thrilled to simply be connecting with Him. It stopped being about, "What can I get from You, God?" and became, "How much time can I give just to have a connection with You?"

We found our perspective on our clients changing too. We started wanting to serve people for the sake of serving them, not because of what we could get from them. We have developed a passion for excellence in all that we do, doing our very best for those who come through our doors and into our lives because we genuinely care about them, whether they become clients or not.

JESUS HAS BECOME OUR CONFIDANT AND OUR MENTOR.

God has blessed our business. Last year our assets and client load doubled, and we are on track this year to double again.

But it's what He has done in our hearts and in our perspectives that has transformed us. Jesus has become our confidant and our mentor. He is a safe place. He is a source of guidance for us, for our family, and for our business. Everything we have today is because of His impact on us. Jesus is just amazing.

—Randy & Arwen

What is the focal
point of our lives?
Is it self?
Is it our efforts?
Is it our good deeds?
Or is it Jesus?

I have observed something else under the sun. The fastest runner doesn't always win the race, and the strongest warrior doesn't always win the battle. The wise sometimes go hungry, and the skillful are not necessarily wealthy. And those who are educated don't always lead successful lives. It is all decided by chance, by being in the right place at the right time.

—Ecclesiastes 9:11

When we are in awe of Jesus, when we recognize His preeminence, we discover the meaning of life. When we are in awe of Jesus, it's amazing how uncomplicated life can be. Life makes more sense when we don't make it about ourselves.

"The Spirit of the Lord is upon me, for he has anointed me to bring Good News to the poor. He has sent me to proclaim that captives will be released, that the blind will see, that the oppressed will be set free, and that the time of the Lord's favor has come."

—Luke 4:18–19

Jesus said over and over that He came for the broken, the bad, the addicted, the bound, the deceived, the lost, the hurting.

WE SERVE HIS FRIENDS

I grew up in a Christian home with parents who were involved in ministry. But in my late teens I rejected all of it as legalistic and walked away. I did my own thing for a while, and I ended up extremely broken and empty. Finally I realized that I really needed God in my life. I rededicated my life to Him and discovered the unconditional love of Jesus.

I DID MY OWN THING FOR A WHILE, AND I ENDED UP EXTREMELY BROKEN AND EMPTY.

I moved around quite a bit after that and eventually ended up in an amazing local church. For the first time, I feel like I have a home. I've found a community of people where we can all feel safe. We can just be who we are. Sometimes we disagree with each other, but we still accept each other as we are and love each other.

When I started getting involved in service projects at church, it was like I'd finally found my calling in life. I remember even as a child feeling like I was called to something bigger than what I was doing every day, but I didn't know what it was until now. I am called to help others and to love others. It just comes out naturally. It's what I live for.

I get to be the hands and feet of Jesus. It's not my calling to drag people into the church. Instead I get to take Jesus *out* to the community. And I love that. I was never meant to live life just for myself. I was meant to live it for others.

—Julia

I AM CALLED TO HELP OTHERS AND TO LOVE OTHERS. I GET TO BE THE HANDS AND FEET OF JESUS.

Being a Christian is not about being good.
It's about relationship.
About grace.
About Jesus.
Jesus is the point of life.

Be strong in the grace that is in Christ Jesus.

—2 Timothy 2:1 NKJV

Jesus fulfills the law for us. When we put our faith in Him, we are made righteous. We can't drum up enough willpower to be perfect, and we don't have to. Jesus already did. . . . Jesus is infinitely righteous, and we are as righteous as He is. So any attempt to make ourselves more righteous by our good deeds would be like trying to one-up infinity.

"The Son of Man came to seek and save those who are lost."

—Luke 19:10

Jesus summed up
His life mission:
"I'm here to find
and help lost
people. That's
why I've come."

I AM AFRAID

Failure after failure in my life had caused me to develop severe anxiety disorder. I've been to more therapy sessions than there are hairs on my head and have been prescribed numerous medications.

But nothing seemed to help. Finally, after losing my job (the failure that broke the camel's back), I became a recluse. I was a healthy young woman who was terrified to leave her apartment. I couldn't even walk my dogs twenty feet from my front door.

I spent a lot of money asking professionals to tell me why I was this way and what was wrong with me. It felt like no one could help. For six months, I was hidden—a recluse and a failure with no answers.

Then I read *Jesus Is _____*. My mind was blown. The moment I understood grace, my heart exploded with an immense joyfulness I had never felt before.

THE MOMENT I UNDERSTOOD GRACE, MY HEART EXPLODED WITH AN IMMENSE JOYFULNESS I HAD NEVER FELT BEFORE.

I realized that the reason I am afraid to even go to the mailbox is this: I am too hard on myself about my failures, real and imagined. It's so simple yet so powerful. There is no reason for me to carry so much weight.

So now when I imagine my list of failures, I picture "Relationship with Jesus" crossed off that list. And when that one is crossed off, the rest of the list just disappears.

Today I went to a personal trainer. Outside. Away from my apartment. And after that, I walked to the grocery store.

That's right. It may sound small, but to me those activities are the equivalent of going skydiving—except this time, I have a parachute that cannot fail.

—Deanna

You can go to bed without fear; you will lie down and sleep soundly.

—Proverbs 3:24

We will never be at rest as long as we are carrying the burden of trying to please God by our good deeds. That is as impossible as it is unnecessary. Jesus was the only one who could, and He already did it, so we need to learn to rest in His completed work.

"This is the will of God, that I should not lose even one of all those he has given me, but that I should raise them up at the last day."

—John 6:39

Jesus is not your accuser. He's not your prosecutor. He's not your judge. He's your friend and your rescuer.

I'm a police officer in Seattle. Recently I responded to a call at a sporting goods store. Dispatch said a guy was trying to use fraudulent credit cards and had provided a fake ID. When I arrived, I could see that the guy was clearly ready to either fight me or flee, but I was able to calm him down enough that I could at least get his ID.

Just then my backup arrived, at which point the suspect decided it was a good idea to bolt. He lunged for the front door, and I sprinted after him. As he fled, I saw him reach into his waistband and realized he was grabbing for a weapon. I managed to tackle him, and as he hit the ground a gun flew out of his hand and landed on the concrete.

I handcuffed him and put him in my patrol car. Then I felt God telling me that I needed to show compassion to the man. I fought that feeling. This guy had just tried to kill me! But the urging didn't go away.

GRACE IS UNDERSERVED, UNEARNED FAVOR.

I didn't know what to say or how to start, so I just asked him what was really going on in his life. For whatever reason, he opened up to me about his past, his family, and his struggles. He was a convicted felon, and he knew that this gun charge meant he was looking at ten years in jail.

GRACE IS A PERSON. GRACE IS JESUS CHRIST.

I didn't know what to say, so I asked if I could pray for him. I looked at him in the rearview mirror. As he sat there in his handcuffs, tears began to stream down his cheeks. He told me he needed that, so I prayed a simple prayer for him.

Then I felt prompted to ask him if he wanted to accept Jesus into his heart. He did, and there in the police car we prayed together before he went inside the jail.

He looked at me right before going inside and said, "Hey, why me? I was going to try to kill you."

JESUS CALLS US TO SHOW HIS LOVE AND HIS GRACE.

"I don't know, man. I don't have a good answer for you," I replied. "But that's what grace is." I told him grace is undeserved, unearned favor. It floored him. He just kept crying, telling me he had experienced Jesus' peace.

I am constantly learning the message of grace. My pastor points people to Jesus and says that grace is a *person*. Grace is Jesus Christ. I just try to apply that every single day on the job.

Jesus calls us to show His love and His grace so that God can become God to others just as He is God to us.

—Jayce

"Let the one who has never sinned throw the first stone!"

—John 8:7

When it comes to sin, the only one who has a right to condemn others is Jesus. And He refused.

"Here on earth you will have many trials and sorrows. But take heart, because I have overcome the world."

—John 16:33

Jesus is more
real, more
present, more
alive, and more
united with us
than we know.

WE NEED THE IMPOSSIBLE

Two days after my wife and I returned from our honeymoon, we were rear-ended at a traffic light. When I tried to get out of the car, I realized something was wrong. My legs weren't following me.

It turned out I had broken my back. I was taken to the hospital, where the doctors told me there was no hope that I would ever walk again. I went home in a wheelchair.

My wife and I began to pray for my healing. One month later, while I was trying to maneuver myself out of the bath on my own, I fell flat on my back. Suddenly I realized I could feel pain in my legs for the first time since my accident. God had healed me—right then.

But six years later, I had a severe allergic reaction to a medication that triggered major seizures. The seizures damaged my back again, and I had to return to the hospital for surgery. When I came out of anesthesia, I had no feeling in one of my legs.

GOD HAD HEALED ME— RIGHT THEN. I spent a month in that hospital, and by the end of my stay, the doctors again told me I would never walk. I replied that I had a better doctor and He would heal me.

For the next six months I remained paralyzed. I was mobile only with the help of three braces, a cane, and my wheelchair. Even though I'd been healed once before, at times I still struggled with doubts as to whether God would do it again. I would sit in church just praying, *God, please heal me. Help me. I can't see the future or when this is going to end. Walk through it with me.*

And He did! Three months ago in a prayer service, several people were praying for me when I realized I could feel my hip again. They kept praying, and I started to feel sensation in my knee and then down to my foot. That night I walked out of church on my own.

I don't need braces or my cane to walk anymore. Recently, I started training for a 5K run. I'm going with friends who have prayed for me and encouraged me through this whole process.

It is all just awesome. I know that Jesus is in all of this. When I was in the wheelchair He carried me. Then He put me back down on the ground and let me walk.

—Alex

You can take my stuff. You can take my position. You can even take my family. But you cannot take Jesus away from me. He is in my heart. His awesomeness, His majesty, His sufficiency, His love for me— those things will last for eternity. He is the ultimate meaning in this life and the life to come.